Copyright © 2018 by Alex Aráez
All rights reserved.

Book and jacket design by Alex Aráez
Book Editing by Toni Bellanca

THE ELEPHANTS UNDER THE RUG

10 Reasons To Go Freelance As A Graphic Designer

Alex Aráez

* Portions of this book were previously published in:
Survive the corporate world and go freelance as a creative designer.

Where the
hell is Viktor?

I think he hasn't
come back from
holidays yet

What? He was supposed to
be here yesterday! We have a
presentation that needs to be
finished tonight…

Preface

I lost all my enthusiasm, and I didn't know why.

I used to be one of those unbearable people that can't stop talking about design. I remember spending my little savings on buying design books when I was just a student. While everyone else was looking forward to going out and get wasted, I was looking forward to reading the next book or going to the upcoming design conference. My friends and family couldn't believe how I changed from being lost in life to being entirely focused on only one thing. Some people told me I was obsessed.

Back in those days, everything was possible. I had plenty to learn and nothing to lose. I managed to be one of those guys who could sell anything to anyone, even though I didn't have any sales in my background. I was able to make analogies on the spot, linking life situations with design or communication. Some people even told me things like: "you should write a book," "you will go far," or "you should be a teacher." I was only in design for a couple of years; I knew nothing. But I spoke passionately, and I believed in what I was saying, and that confidence perhaps made people believe in me.

I had a promising future. I had a great job. I had made it – some people would say. But all that was far from the truth.

One day, all of a sudden, all my enthusiasm was gone. My passion went away like smoke on a windy day.

I lost what kept me going for so many years. I lost what excited me and what woke me up at night. I had no enthusiasm for any particular job or design project. I quit my job and locked myself at home for four months, where I did nothing. I felt empty.

I got sick any time I thought about coming back to work. I was exhausted. And worst of all, I had no idea why.

Everyone knew one thing about me: I was a passionate designer. But, to me, it was a confusing period because I wasn't that person anymore. I stopped caring about design or creativity. The industry had become toxic, and it made me feel tired and the opposite of excited.

It was hard to admit to the people around me. I merely said I needed rest. I honestly hoped that my passion would come back. That I will be on fire again and that it was just a 'down period'. But it wasn't.

Months went by, and nothing changed. Years went by, and nothing changed. Believe it or not, it took me nearly six years to get out of it and to finally understand what the hell happened.

I had a burnout. In 2012, I had a massive burnout. But I didn't have any clarity on what was happening to me. I guess I quit my job before I blew up. And since I wasn't able to admit it to myself, I couldn't get any help to get out of it. I had no information about what a burnout is and how to deal with it.

Instead, I just let time heal and hoped for the best. But what I did wrong was to force myself to keep working to maintain my image of being a designer. Which, in turn, made me drag the burnout out for all those years.

I couldn't go back to a full-time job, so I decided to go freelance and see what my chances were. At least I would be my own boss, and I could take time off anytime I wanted. I worked on many projects, and literally, none of them excited me as in my early days. I thought it would never be the same.

Until one day I got a severe physical injury that didn't allow me to work.

I had an operation in my right shoulder, and I couldn't work for over four months. I couldn't open my computer; I could hardly use my phone. My days were about going for walks, having coffee on terraces and reading books. I had plenty of time.

It's funny how incredibly slow time passes when you have nothing to do. Those four months felt like a year. Since I was physically incapacitated, I couldn't distract myself with sports or any other activities. My only distractions were friends, food, books and being in my head, thinking.

That period was the time of healing. Not just for my shoulder, but for everything. Even my burnout. It was the first time I realized that I just had a burnout and I didn't deal with it appropriately. That I was resisting it and I was afraid of admitting to myself and others that I wasn't the same passionate person anymore.

When I admitted this to myself, it felt like fresh air. I felt like I unplugged something that was stuck. I had clarity at last.

A burnout doesn't happen in one day. It happens slowly, bit by bit. Those bits that led to my burnout and what many creatives face in their day to day are what I call 'Elephants' – The obvious problems most companies decide to ignore or put 'under the rug'.

I have met other people who burned out as well. Some of them were severely damaged and needed to visit a psychologist to deal with the problem. Some others decided to travel the world and find inspiration somewhere. And many others either started their own companies or became freelancers, as I did.

I can say I am back in the industry again, but I learned to protect my mental health. Now, I negotiate some conditions before I work anywhere, especially in advertising. It turns out that now is the best time of my creative career. Ideas are now flying. It's almost effortless. I let creativity come to me naturally. I spent little time on the computer and more on the notebook. I keep a healthy work/life balance, and that is noticeable in the work I produce.

I am also working on personal projects, which are the ones I enjoy the most and the ones that keep me awake, like writing and designing books like this one.

The Elephants Under the Rug is a wake-up call to an industry constantly evolving on the outside, but stuck on the inside. It points out some of the most common problems the creative industry faces internally. The ones that make talented people leave or burn out. The ones about poor creative work, inefficiency, employee mental health, unsustainable workloads, and big egos, among others.

I wrote this book hoping to do two things: prevent talented creatives from getting overworked into a burnout, and offer some realistic encouragement to those who might enjoy becoming independent as a freelancer. To do that, I'm just going to tell the truth. I'm going to say what many people can't – or won't – say. Because you need to hear it.

Maybe you're a creative on an internal corporate or agency team. Or perhaps you're a freelancer trying to find your footing and a strong direction. Either way, the grass probably sometimes looks greener on the other side. You sometimes wonder about making the switch, or wonder if you'll regret having already made it.

But the truth is, both sides come with their own elephants. It's your job to decide which ones you can live with.

To Viktor,
who never finished
that presentation.

For deciding to never
come back to that office
again and for politely
telling his boss
to go fuck himself.

CONTENTS

Part one
–
ELEPHANTS IN THE CREATIVE INDUSTRY
Ten reasons why designers go freelance.

01. Too many opinions	16
02. Big egos	21
03. Revolving doors	23
04. Overtime	25
05. Interruptions	29
06. Meetings	32
07. Micromanagement	34
08. Multitasking	35
09. Leadership	38
10. Where the money goes	42

Part two
—

ELEPHANTS IN THE FREELANCE BUSINESS

No one said being a freelancer was smooth sailing.

Going freelance	48
Presenting yourself	51
Presenting your work	59
Presenting your work to a client.	59
Presenting your work online.	62
Quoting	65
Approaching companies	68
Letting them find you	72
Recruitment agencies	74
Big brands	77
Scarcity	80
ASAP	82
The startup promise	87
Quality, not quantity	90
Skinny dogs, bad taste and relationships.	94

Part three
—

CHOOSING YOUR ELEPHANTS

"It isn't for me."	100
"I can't go back to a full-time job anymore."	101
Choose your elephants	102
Your two cents	105

Part one
—
ELEPHANTS IN THE CREATIVE INDUSTRY

Ten reasons why designers go freelance.

01.
Too many opinions

Have you ever played that game where a bunch of people sit in a circle, and the first person whispers a secret into the ear of the person next to them, then that person whispers it to the next, and the message goes around the circle? In the end, it ends up being an entirely different secret. It's called 'The telephone game' or 'Chinese whispers'.

In big companies, opinions come from left and right. Your work will have to pass through a labyrinth of layers and opinions to get to the last approval or the final decision-maker. And by the time an original, good idea reaches the decision-maker, it's become so different that it probably no longer makes sense. Or if it does, it might at the very least have suffered from everyone adding in their two cents.

Democracy, even though it can be a beautiful idea, does not work in communication. The idea of choosing something democratically may sound good in a political campaign, but not everyone is equally talented or has the same background.

Only the people who have been working on a problem long enough have the knowledge and intelligence to propose ideas considering all angles.

I have been in presentations in which a project manager commented on not liking a feature or an idea. I have heard people coming from a financial background saying "that idea won't work." I have heard "this font is ugly," from someone whose role was business accounts.

Just because you have eaten food before doesn't entitle you to tell Jamie Oliver how to cook a stew.

Opinions, on the other hand, are well received when they come with tact. I used to work with one brand manager who was quite tough, but he knew how to share his opinion. He always said: "I am not a designer, I have no idea of how to do this, and this is your call... but from a marketing point of view, perhaps our audience... etc."

That point of view has no commitment. He allows us to ignore it if we want, it's still our call, as it should be. He knows he can't tell us how to do our jobs. We all respected that guy because he respected us.

Showing respect for the people who have been working on a project for a long time should be mandatory.

Unfortunately, the brand manager I used to work with is a rare gem, and many people in the creative industry have a long way to go when it comes to giving opinions.

I remember once being in a situation of having to sell something I thought was insulting to any human being with half a brain. The original proposal was exciting, but after all people's opinions and changes, it turned into a really stupid solution. I didn't want to defend something I didn't believe in, especially since the CEO of the company was really intelligent and had an excellent sense for communication.

I had to present it anyway, and all I felt was embarrassment. The CEO wasn't convinced, and I agreed with all she said and had nothing positive to say. Knowing there was a significant possibility of me getting fired, I mentioned the original idea. "We did think of a different solution at first," I said. After two seconds of intensity from everyone except the CEO, she said that she would love to go ahead with that idea. Luckily, since I had said 'we' instead of 'I', everyone was happy to make the adjustments, share the credit and let it go.

This situation was the exception and not the rule. When everyone in a company gives opinions, an original, great idea will get twisted beyond recognition during the approval phases. And this is one of the biggest frustrations of creative people, and what leads them to leave companies.

Creativity and design are talents that take years or decades to master. It is not for everyone, despite what many people believe. And this constant back-and-forth of opinions makes the process endless. It exhausts the creative team, resulting in massive quotes and poor creative work.

But I can offer one small glimmer of hope. Remember that original idea? The one the purely expressed your vision and ideal? Save that version for your portfolio. Because that one is a much more explicit expression of your creativity than the 'final piece' that gets printed, published or posted.

"Your opinions are well noted." – This is a way to respond to opinions that don't matter.

"It's their idea"

02.
Big egos

It was Friday around 6pm when we finished the project. We thought we made it. We thought it would look beautiful in stores. We were the only ones in the office, and we only had to make a phone call to get it approved worldwide.

The Creative Director didn't need anybody in between, so she went ahead and called the CEO directly.

The CEO gladly invited us to come upstairs. She welcomed us, and we showed her the project. It was just the three of us, it was cozy, and we all enjoyed talking and presenting it casually.

It took about ten minutes, and the CEO congratulated us for making such a beautiful project in such a tight deadline. She approved without hesitation. It became a global solution.

We left her office looking forward to sharing it internally on Monday. It was a huge success.

Was it? To our surprise, our action made many people angry. We went against the rules. The rules said to share first with everyone in the department before it goes to the CEO.

We were shocked. We managed to do a large project in little time, we got it approved by the CEO, and it looked great, why did people get so upset?

We had a couple of internal meetings where we had to explain ourselves. We were asked to come up with revisions when it was already approved. We got warned never to do this again. The funniest thing about it all is that these people had no background in design and their ideas were ridiculous. They were at the same company stuck for ages, and they had no other way to demonstrate their authority.

It was the biggest bunch of nonsense and display of egos I have ever seen.

People with big egos need to put a dent on every project to prove their worthiness. They need to feel as if it was their idea, not yours.

In the end, the project went ahead as we presented it, as much as everyone hated us. It got many compliments in all countries, and the CEO came downstairs to congratulate us all, including our 'friends' in the marketing department.

03.
Revolving doors

My father used to run a business that was very successful. He used to be an expert in his field. He didn't study architecture, but he knew how to build things. He was committed, persistent and ambitious. His appreciation for his people made him a great leader. I know this well, since I worked in his company as a teenager, and I could see how the employees respected him. They told me stories about how well he managed all situations, and what a good person he was.

The business grew over the years and became known in the industry at a national level. Friends and family were very important to my father, and he hired many of them because he is a kind person who wanted to help other people. When I was working there, it seemed like every employee was either a neighbor or family member.

For many years, this all went well. But then the economic crisis hit. To survive, my father needed the support and understanding of his employees. Something he thought would happen naturally, since he literally saved some of them from poverty.

Well, guess what? Even our relatives ended up suing my father. Because when the money was gone, so was the relationship. They didn't care. They were only thinking of themselves, and when it came to them having to give us something, then it was: "fuck you! I'll sue you even if you are my uncle."

Leaders and business owners very often face the uncomfortable situation of a relative or a friend asking them for employment. As in my father's story, it can easily lead to a disaster. But the social pressure is so high that often, to avoid conflicts or disappoint family, we put people in positions for which they are probably not qualified.

This also applies to promotions - have you ever wondered why so many politicians are where they are when they don't have any merit for it? In my country, this leads to a problem we call the 'revolving doors' – people who go from being Minister of Defense to Minister of Health, and one year later Minister of Culture – while not being any good at any of them.

Organizations are run by people and being social, and building relationships is more important than anything else. This principle affects the vast majority of organizations we know, from small businesses to entire governments.

Good or bad, in the end, it is all a matter of connections, not talent. The companies for which you work (or worked, or will work) are no different. Many companies in the creative industry are filled with 'friends'. Being kind to others is a must, but I believe that being in a position of power should be earned by being an inspiring professional, not by being friends with the guys on top. Remember this when things are not making much sense. It usually is the result of revolving doors.

04.
Overtime

How did yesterday go?

*Great... we stayed until 5am,
back at the office at 9am...
Really tired but we made it!*

*Wow, dude, that sucks!
And they still made you come
to the office today?*

It was around the 1850s when countries first started to apply the eight-hour workday, and that was only after many brave people confronted the system of the time. It took decades of real effort, pain, and commitment from these people who stood up against unfair labor conditions.

And here we are in the 21st century, working all night long, doing whatever it takes to make the company we work for reach 'success'. We get briefs and meetings placed at 6pm when everyone is supposed to go home. We get emails on weekends and invitations to presentations on Sunday. It's like the companies we work for are submissive to the client's requests, and our life outside the office means nothing.

When young creatives are still studying, their enthusiasm leads them to believe just about anything on how to build a career. Especially the belief that you 'have to work hard to get somewhere'. While that is true, the problem begins when people confuse 'working hard' with 'working overtime'.

Usually, our focus and productivity are very high for the first four to six hours of the day. The rest of the hours we spend in the office are just fillers. Which means that working overtime is counter-productive.

If you are steady throughout the week, and you maintain a high level of focus in the hours when you are productive, you will get more done than anyone working long hours.

The morning after a long and exhausting night at work develops as follows:

Get to the office around 9:30 or 10pm. Get a large coffee to wake up. Check your emails. Answer some of them. Go to the bathroom. Meet someone in between. Chit chat about yesterday's marathon. Go to the kitchen again for another coffee. More chit-chat. Get back to your desk. Sit down. Check your WhatsApp messages. Answer them. Join the conversation of your colleagues about whatever they are talking about. Someone calls a meeting in 10 minutes. Those 10 minutes are not enough to get anything done. Open Facebook. Scroll down engaging with nothing. Go to the meeting. Sit and feel the comfortable chair. Fight to not fall asleep while someone shares some random charts. Finish the meeting. Time to start to work. Oops, it's lunchtime.

If you were working all night, you depleted your energy, and whatever you are doing in the morning will be done on auto-pilot. You won't be creative. Or you won't deliver anything of value. And it makes sense. Your energy levels are in the negative. You are hoping to leave today and get some good rest, but someone puts you on a meeting at 6pm, and the cycle starts again.

This is the cycle of inefficiency that is generated every week at most advertising agencies. Old-school agencies that aim to win awards and pitches, but that don't value the well-being of their employees.

I have worked in other companies where things were really different. Everyone left at 6pm without even saying goodbye. They left, period. What can't be done today, will be done tomorrow.

I remember some of the great managers I had in the past. When someone from another department tried to take a shortcut and go

OVERTIME OVER

directly to me, I saw my manager blocking the path that led to my desk, and with a big smile telling this person to go back and make an appointment with her first. They were not allowed to bother the creative team.

No one came to interrupt. I could do great work, and no one asked me to stay long hours. The company had values, and they were clear from the first day. "It's important you take one hour for lunch, and go home at 6pm, we want you rested," I was told on my first day.

We were never late, we produced great creative work, and we felt good. And it was at one of the most-known brands worldwide.

The fact that an agency is well-known, too busy, or has many awards to win, doesn't mean they can't have values.

A lack of values is not an excuse; it's a choice. So is overtime.

I remember saying that once in an elevator, all the people looking at me like I said something that was not allowed because in theory it is supposed to be a cool thing to work hard and in 20-hour shifts to make things happen.

But I continued: "How does your company expect you to be happy and creative if they ask you to give up your life for a presentation no one cares about?"

Their faces revealed thoughts of something in between "who the fuck is this guy?" and "he is right, and my life is miserable."

05.
Interruptions

Imagine you are trying to sleep. But every ten minutes, someone interrupts you just to check if you are sleeping. Tell me, how do you think you'll feel the next morning?

To get the beneficial effects of sleep, we need to enter the different REM cycles, and it's only after three or four hours that we are really resting, eliminating toxins and refreshing our bodies.

Creativity is like sleeping. It works the same way. It requires concentration, research, and immersion in your thoughts to get to something interesting. It's only after long periods of focus that you get to a real understanding of a problem, to something.

This important fact is what most companies forget because they are run by old management systems, and they apply the same concepts to all departments.

How often do you get interrupted? Do you feel that some days you get nothing done? Have you been bouncing from one meeting room to another and not doing anything productive?

On a typical day, we are continuously interrupted, in the form of emails, phone calls, small talk, social media, etc. And if that's not enough, we also have the daily routines of the office environment. There is a common belief that you have to be social in a company. That concept can help your career, but it can also become a problem when it becomes socializing for socializing's sake.

There is a time for being social and a time for being productive. When you interrupt a colleague to see how things are going, your intentions are probably friendly, but you might be interrupting his process or his 'creative REM cycle'. Something you could have done in the kitchen or during lunch.

More often than not, you'd be really lucky to get one hour of interruption-free concentration in an office, because if it's not a phone call or a meeting, one of your colleagues will come to your desk to ask what are you working on.

In creativity, this does NOT work. This causes many problems, from shitty ideas that are poorly executed to long hours at the office trying to come up with something that can be done in less time with the proper thinking and concentration.

The only times I could come up with good ideas – the ones I put in my portfolio – were on weekends, and when I was at home. After having a long and delicious breakfast, without having to go anywhere. Having to report to no one and letting my ideas flow without pressure.

This is also why open-plan offices often don't work at all. We work better when we choose when to get interrupted, but in today's offices, where everyone is allowed to interrupt each other, it's nearly impossible to get any work done.

It's no wonder why remote workers are popular for being the most efficient.

HEY... ARE YOU SLEEPING?

06.
Meetings

I have been in meetings listening to people talking about how expensive yesterday's groceries were, the funny things their cat did over the weekend, and how wasted they ended up last Saturday.

Meetings may be necessary for some, but, for us creatives, the majority of meetings are really unproductive gatherings that lead nowhere. If you are a Creative Director, Art Director, Strategist, Designer or the like, you might have experienced the frustration of always being stuck in meetings and not doing what you are hired to do: produce creative work. Meetings force us to switch our concentration to something that probably has very little to do with our main priority. It is very easy to get distracted in an office routine, and very hard to maintain actual concentration to produce something of value. And regular meetings don't help, they only interrupt.

Here are some common meetings you'll sit through when you're in a creative team, and what to watch out for:

WORKLOAD MEETINGS

A meeting necessary for management. The problem is when managers involve the creative team too when this isn't necessary for the entire meeting. It's much more efficient to only invite the creative to the point in the meeting in which you're talking about creative work.

I have been in many workload meetings, and I wasted most of my time listening to other people's notes when, first, I only needed two minutes to explain what my workload status was and, second, I don't have to know what other people are working on.

BRAINSTORMING SESSIONS

If you have been in one of these, you know the drill: people start by saying something related to the project, then someone cracks a joke, everyone laughs, and most of the people relax and wait for others to contribute. Brainstorming sessions might work for some, but my theory on this is that it's a matter of personality and whether you are more of an introverted or an extroverted person. Extroverted people can do well in brainstorm sessions, while introverted people don't. Instead, they need time alone and to concentrate on coming up with good ideas.

Still, I believe that the bigger the group, the bigger the distraction. I love brainstorming sessions when I am tired, and I have nothing urgent to do - it is an excellent way to laugh with your colleagues. On the other hand, I always avoid them when I need to get things done. To be honest, I think that brainstorming sessions are a waste of time, and I never saw a good idea coming from them.

MANAGER CHECKS

Another form of interruption is when managers come to your desk to 'check'. This is another unnecessary layer on top of all the layers we already have, and another distraction and break of focus.

I have worked with great managers who only saw the presentation when it was presented to marketing, and they always managed everything perfectly. They were brilliant at dealing with my assistance to meetings, marking it as optional.

When I skip most meetings, I am able to focus and produce good work. And the best of it all is that I never miss anything important, which makes me think most meetings are not necessary.

"Meetings are for people who don't have enough to do." - Paul Arden.

07.
Micromanagement

It's funny that still today many people believe in the old-school assumption that you have to be there, in front of the computer, to actually 'work'.

You can spend days in front of the computer hoping to find inspiration and only get mediocre ideas that anyone could come up with. While you could disconnect, do something else and find inspiration somewhere else. I got the best ideas while I was joking with friends or doing something that had nothing to do with the work itself. Sometimes, taking a break can end up saving you days of work.

I have worked for companies strictly remotely, even being in the same country. I have never been to their offices, we communicated by phone and email, and our relationship has been great. Exciting creative work, no nonsense or wasting time on meetings. They trusted me, and I delivered before we hit the deadline. Some days, I got booked to work three days on something, but it took me a few hours to come up with the concept, and a few hours to put it all together. Some others, I struggled for days more than the time I estimated, but in the end, it all came together. Our relationship was based on results, not on being present or in front of the computer, pretending I am working.

Micromanagement is just someone's insecurity. It makes people don't feel trusted. It's irritating. And it's counter-productive.

08.
Multitasking

Stop lying to yourselves: multitasking is the archenemy of productivity.

I have worked with many 'multitaskers' in my career. Usually, they are young people in their 20s. They think that they are doing well with the million tasks they accomplish every day, but they forget that most of these little tasks are non-productive and end up being a waste of everyone's time.

The result of working this way is that we always end up waiting for hours for files to be delivered, or for the things that really matter that get lost in their queue. Then they complain about the long hours of work and exhaustion and say non-stop: "There's so much work to do!" and "I am so busy!" And a few minutes later, they are answering some random message on Facebook. It makes me laugh.

When you multitask, what your brain is doing is stopping its concentration on your current task, re-orientating its attention to a different one, and concentrating again on developing the new task. When you switch, the same process happens again: interrupt, re-orientate, re-develop.

This happens even with smaller distractions, like checking your phone or answering that text message. It might seem like you only spent 30 seconds on it, but breaking your concentration and fixing it again requires a lot of time and energy. Most importantly, it doesn't let you dig deep into any one task.

The ability to focus and get things done is an undervalued quality that nowadays is hard to find.

I got hired by an agency once to work on a branding project that had been difficult for them to crack. I had a meeting with the Creative

Director before I accepted the job, to discuss with him the conditions of my temporary contract.

I told him I have the ability to focus and I am usually faster than average without compromising quality. I explained to him my thoughts about creativity, meetings, and overtime I described previously in the book.

They were fantastic to me. They put me with a great project manager who protected me from useless meetings or unnecessary requests, they allowed me to sit in a quiet room in the building, and they trusted me to share my work when I had something, without anyone checking behind my shoulder.

I was hired for a month. I finished my work in three days. And spent another few days developing another project. The rest of time was wasted between people who had no clue of what they had to do. Because they were too busy multitasking.

The one who embraces a lot holds nothing.

Famous saying.

09.
Leadership

"Next time, be more organized with your files."

That was one of the comments a colleague of mine got from a production manager who forgot to organize the files herself, which was actually her job.

My colleague was busy bouncing back a forth from one meeting to another to 'plan' what to do next to get the project moving forward. He was the pivotal person within the company for every decision that involved creative work. His work was more of a messenger than a creative person.

He told me that everyone was complaining about how things should be done, but no one was doing anything to fix them.

Everyone was blaming one another, and it was no one's fault.

The chaos in that company was unbearable. The roles within the team were blurred. The tasks each of us had to do were not delivered on time. And the accounts team were promising the client presentations we were not doing. No one was communicating internally, and the project was a mediocre idea, it was horribly executed, and it was poorly presented.

Supposing everyone is doing his or her job properly, the Creative Director is the one to blame for all this mess, not the individuals who are lost in translation. The director is the one who defines the roles and establishes who delivers what.

I consider myself lucky for having worked with a few great leaders.

I had once a great Creative Director who was passionate about creativity and good work. When our team got a new project, she would know exactly which lines of exploration to go for. She directed the team creatively, something I hardly ever see.

She was also fierce about protecting her team above everything else. I remember several occasions when some people requested changes to a proposal based on their taste and with no explanation, and her answer was always something along the lines of "We appreciate your ideas, but we disagree, and this stays as-is for now."

Many people didn't like her; other people loved her. That's what happens when you stand up for something: you will get followers and haters. But as a result of her attitude, we had a clear creative direction and objectives, we produced excellent work in very efficient timeframes, the company was getting great communication campaigns, and we were happy.

I have also worked in a small studio with another great Creative Director. He was very relaxed and always making sketches - all visual. He always took into account the communications and the practical side of everything, with an excellent eye for design - although he didn't design anything himself. He was good at helping us find a clear direction in our projects, and when requesting something, he questioned us like this: "Wouldn't it be stronger if we say it this way?"

These experiences taught me that a great leader makes a big difference. The problem is when a leader confuses the idea of leadership with being hard for no reason, imposing authority, or continuously reminding their people who is in charge.

I worked at another agency where the Creative Director was a nightmare. His first problem was a lack of tact. He treated people well some days, badly on others. He was one of those mood-changers, I never knew what I was going to get the next time.

His second problem was a lack of direction. He was good at design, but not in creative direction. He never directed any project from the start. Instead, he had a habit of showing up when the project was already presented to the client, and he would then want to change everything no matter what. All these changes were often requested after 6pm, or on Friday end of the day, meaning the team would have to work the whole weekend. I got the feeling it was all done on purpose.

Because of all of this, the creative team in that office would change every month, with new people coming in and other people burning out and leaving. The result was that the creative work was poor and chaotic, and the vibe in that office was hell on earth.

And another problem I see is when the Creative Director is there to make everyone happy and not stand for anything. That was the case of the first company I explained at the beginning of the chapter. And look how well it ended, everyone complaining about each other without any clear direction of what to do to make things work.

Leadership is about inspiring and helping teams navigate smoothly and efficiently, not to make friends or impose authority.

From what I have seen and learned, here are some tips to make yourself into a great leader. And to create a more healthy, positive and productive environment in a creative company:

- Except for some rare occasions, everyone leaves the office at 6pm (go back to the chapter on overtime to understand how important this is). Let your team have a life and get inspired outside the office.
- Accept only the work that you, as a company, are capable of delivering at the highest quality possible, without relying on the creative team's overtime and weekends.
- Cut down the old hierarchy systems. If design has to sell the idea to a client, ask design to work together with the client

and remove all layers in between. It is easier said than done, but it is possible.
- Reduce meetings to a minimum: leave that for management, not for the creative team.
- Avoid the every-day 'checks', no matter how important the project is. Your team are not children, and if you give them space, they will deliver.
- Avoid big groups of brainstorming sessions. Instead, ask them to go in teams of two to have a coffee outside the office with pen and paper.
- Establish some code, in which people are allowed to do their work for the first four or five hours of the day with no interruptions. Let the meetings, phone calls, and other miscellanea happen at the end of the day.
- Avoid open spaces when possible, and let your people have some privacy or work remotely. They will perform better since they will feel trusted.

By applying some of these rules, your company's productivity will increase, and your team will feel better about their work. If you as a leader can apply all of them, your team's energy and the quality of the work will skyrocket.

10.

Where the money goes

When working on a design project, you could go on a big scale and spend millions, or be creative and spend little.

The difference between a project that relies on a budget or a project that requires people use money more wisely can be enormous. I recently did the marketing material and a campaign for a new book launch. The campaign was based on photographic still-life imagery, using female human hands, bright colors, and oversized elements. We also needed punchy copy lines and a strategy to sell it online. We needed to create three main images.

A campaign of this scale can add up to quite a bit of money. If you go all the way up, you would need an art director, a photographer, a photographer assistant, a hand model, a set and prop stylist, and the entire production team. Three images of that scale will take a day or longer. Plus retouching and everything in between. On top of that, we would have to pay usage rights to the photography, which means we could only use them for a limited amount of time. We would also need an excellent creative copywriter to make punchy lines, and probably a web designer to put the website together.

I am not an expert in coming up with these numbers, but using top professionals, this could go up to 30k, if not more.

Guess how much budget we spent doing those? Besides a week of my time, less than €200. Hard to believe, right? We just used resources and made the comps by ourselves. We bought imagery of hands and various elements, and oversized them ourselves. We painted the objects in post-production, and we used the same copywriter who edited the book. The marketing campaign looks stunning, and still, everyone asks: "who did you work with?"

Sometimes the agencies I have worked for can't believe what I am capable of doing. I am not exceptionally talented or gifted. I am just a hands-on Art Director with a graphic design background. I come from backgrounds with little money, where we were taught to create from scratch and to pay attention to resources. Of course, I, too, enjoy working with great professionals and making something happen together. But more often than not, many projects can be solved much quicker, with fewer resources and fewer people involved.

I had a great client once who asked me to create her brand. As a natural part of the brand development, I asked her what she was thinking about the website. She said she was talking to a company that makes sites and she was happy with them so far.

Knowing how things go in this industry, I asked her what they quoted her for such a simple website. She said around 10k. I was shocked.

The same story repeats. You can go all the way up, or spend little to get the same result. I proposed her to do the same for a fraction of that budget. She didn't need much, a simple site with the homepage, about, contact and little more. I designed the site using WordPress and asked a developer from my network to build the site, and make adjustments to her online shop. We did those with woo commerce for WordPress – a free and open-source plugin.

There is also the combo of going all the way up, together with the agency hours, which cost way more than freelancers' hours. The biggest waste of the client's money I have seen is usually when many people are involved in a project.

I have seen teams of about ten people try to develop apps that only needed two people to start. I am not saying the other eight people were not required for the project - they were - but at different phases.

If instead of putting ten people to work on developing a new project from scratch, a company invests first in thinking about it and making a plan to make it happen, the rest will be done much quicker, saving the company and the client a lot of time and cost.

This company used to have a meeting every morning - every. single. morning(!) - a meeting to 'catch up'. These meetings were the most ridiculous I have ever seen.

It was supposed to be in a ten-minute meeting that started at 10am, usually catching me right in the middle of doing something relevant. Ten people had to say what they did the day before and what they were doing today, then the conversation always stretched longer than expected and the meetings would end up lasting between 30 and 45 minutes, sometimes even an hour.

After that, everyone went running to have another cup of coffee or to smoke, which meant that at the end of the day the team only started working at 11; from 9am to 11am, nothing was done. Two hours worth of work for ten people: that is precisely 20 hours of productivity wasted, and 20 hours work at a communications agency is not exactly inexpensive.

When that project was about to end, I remember they wanted to hire me to do another, similar project, and I said sure, but the project can be done conceptually and visually in about five days instead of a month.

How? First, I merely proposed to work together with the strategist on the concept and the design direction by ourselves - without any meetings, web developers or project management. I told them just to give us time to think, and we will make it happen, we will present it to the client. Once it was approved, the execution would be straightforward, because we all know what we are doing.

When I explained this to the technical team, they said that it was all they wanted: to know exactly what is needed when. And to not keep 'trying things out' for the sake of presenting useless prototypes. That was again another case of a filler being used to justify the budget they submitted. In the end, the way of working that I suggested was a win-win for everyone.

Did they accept it? No. It was more profitable to have people wasting time. Here is one sad truth of the advertising world: many agencies need to put in many hours of work to make a profit. When probably they are not needed, or they could be re-invested.

It should go against any company's principles to waste money or resources. Money can be placed somewhere else, but the long hours lost by creatives is never given back to them.

And don't get me wrong, I have also worked for companies who were efficient and practical. That's why I can compare.

Bad planning, lack of creativity and poor execution are the money suckers of our industry. Keep this in mind when negotiating your salary or rates.

Part two
—
ELEPHANTS IN THE FREELANCE BUSINESS

No one said being a freelancer was smooth sailing.

Going freelance

"I can't be a freelancer; I need my safety and my income."

Safety and stability are the main reasons why people don't go out on their own. At the same time, full-time employees think that our life as freelancers can be like a dream, not depending on anyone and taking holidays as we please.

Being a freelancer or having your own business might seem attractive to some, to others it might seem terrifying. And it's ok either way.

If the idea of not having a monthly salary makes you sick, then you should find a job and stick with it. If you want to grow within the business and you are good enough, you will escalate positions until you gain some recognition. You will have about twenty-something days of holiday. You will work eight hours a day, five days a week (if you are lucky), and you will get incremental salary increases the longer you stay. You may even get a pension. Your path is clear.

If on the other hand, you want a different future where you can choose everything for yourself, you have to start freelancing or running your own business. Your path will be unclear: maybe you start and find no work for a year. Or maybe you get lucky and find great clients to work for. Maybe your clients don't pay on time, and you go bankrupt in less than six months. Maybe you discover you are not strong enough to pass the pain period and you start to doubt everything. Which may lead to taking another full-time job with a superior that is less qualified than you are. But maybe, you succeed. All of this is part of the uncertainty that comes with going on your own.

Let's assume you are a risk-taker, a driven and committed person. Right now, let's focus on the issue of financial stability, which is what worries people the most.

The truth is, it's a bad strategy to start as a freelancer without any cash reserves. If you want to sell your services well, you need to appear as though you do not need the clients, even if you do. So you should never look too 'hungry' when you're talking to clients. Your attitude should be: the clients want me. It is a mindset strategy; easier said than done. But there are a few tricks to help create this mentality.

Start by having some savings. It's only common sense. When I worked at my first job, my main goal was to become a freelancer, so I could work directly with clients and set my own rules. Since that was my main goal, I saved as much money as I could, during every full-time job I had. It was the price I paid to be able to do what I wanted, to be able to face worst-case scenarios and survive a few months of not getting paid. In the beginning, it is really easy to accept small and underpaid jobs, but I didn't want that. As my father said: "skinny dogs attract fleas." I wanted the big clients who were willing to pay for high-quality work; otherwise, I would rather go to a full-time job.

Again, it wasn't easy, seven months into my freelancing career, and I had gotten nothing. I felt hopeless. I even registered on online platforms that hire freelancers. The pool of talent there was massive, and the hourly rates were really low, and the clients were always aiming for the cheapest possible designer to make their dreams come true.

I began to doubt everything, and I even considered getting a full-time job again. Finally, around month eight, I got my first client. It took time, but it paid off. All these months are what I've called the pain period.

The pain period is where most people give up in any of the new things they try to do. How many people do you know that join the gym in January with a great workout plan on their minds and don't last a week? They want to get ripped or lose weight, but they don't want to work out. That example is very literal, but also applies to the freelance life: you will get rejected left and right, so be prepared.

This feeling of rejection and failure comes from the outside, too. As you face the pain period, you will feel pressure from your partner, your parents and everyone around you. They'll tell you the decision you made was wrong and that you need to find a job; that quitting was stupid and that you have to do all sorts of things to go back to 'normal'.

They tell you these things because they love you and they want the best for you. The problem is, they don't know what's best for you. Only you do.

So don't listen to what people tell you to do. Their opinions are based on fear, and if they have never been where you are or where you want to be, their perspective is worth nothing. Just listen to the ones who have done it, their advice is based on achievement, and it will be more useful. And they will tell you the same thing I'm telling you now: take the risk. Get off your comfortable chair and go out on your own.

Presenting yourself

If you are considering going freelance, you will have to sell what you can do for others, whether you like it or not.

In an attempt to master everything, some of us start freelancing with a broad offering, trying to know about everything. As much as it may hurt for some to hear, it's a fact that we can't be good at everything or liked by everyone.

I, too, made the mistake of starting with a generic freelance profile where I could offer anything. Soon enough, I started getting requests I didn't enjoy doing. Then I realized that being good at everything was neither productive nor realistic. I was wasting my time and the time of others. So I learned to focus on the things I do well, and leave the rest for my free time.

Defining your profile is about understanding how you well you perform and feel working on certain conditions. And about making clear what you can do for others, which is your contribution.

You can start with performance, or your preferences for the way you work.

But before digging into that, I will share something that made me change my perspective on work environments, as well as my performance.

Where do you fall in the introvert/extrovert spectrum?
This is not the topic of my book, and I am not an expert in this field. But this question changed my perception of so many things, that I have to talk about it.

I have lived my entire life with the wrong perception of what it means to be extroverted or introverted. If you meet me, you will think that I am an extrovert: I'm very social and energetic, I am not shy, and I speak loudly. I thought I was an extrovert too, until a few months back, when I came across an article about their differences. I learned that we all have it wrong.

People associate introversion with shyness, with people who shrink their shoulders and quietly sit in a corner, not speaking to anyone. Fortunately, that's not the case. Introversion has nothing to do with shyness. Shyness is a social anxiety. It's a different concept altogether.

The main difference between being an extrovert or an introvert is how one's energy is generated. Extroverted people get their energy from being around people, while introverts need their time alone to recharge. For introverted people, it's important to spend time alone to concentrate, to make things happen and to think deeply. That's why the modern way of working in open offices may not work for them. That's why brainstorming sessions or meetings are a waste of time for these individuals. That's why some people work better alone rather than in groups.

Some people are more neutral, some people are more extreme cases of one or the other, but creative people tend to be sensitive and fall more on the introversion side, or at least this is what I have experienced. If you recognize something about yourself in this, I invite you to dig more into the subject. At least you will understand the reasons why you do what you do, and what your strong or weak points are. This will help you to deal with them in the future.

Now, knowing where you fall in that spectrum, let's get back to some questions about performance. Have a thought about these; they are not mind-blowing or difficult questions, it is just to help define your work environments better, making you more efficient.

Do you perform better being alone or in groups?
Do prefer open-plan offices or having privacy?
Are you good at the global vision or a skilled professional in details?
What are your strengths? And weaknesses?
What is your ideal role in a company?

Be honest with yourself; this is not about what other people find interesting, it's about where you feel good about your job.

If you are a graphic designer, but you get lost and can't come up with ideas from scratch, then you can present yourself as a technical designer, the one who gets things done and produced.

If, on the contrary, you hate producing, but you are creative, present yourself as a creative graphic designer.

Why is this important? Because in the freelance world, companies are looking for specialists that can solve problems. If they hire you as a creative, but you can't come up with ideas, they will think you are everything but good. They won't call you again, and you will get a bad reputation within that company. Same applies if they think you can produce the PowerPoint presentations, but you are instead a creative designer, and PowerPoints are not your thing. They will think you made them waste their time and money.

It's important to know where you stand. You can make better choices or communicate more clearly, which will make you more effective. And being effective is a good reputation to have, especially if you quote hourly.

Now, that you have a better idea about performance, let's take a look at how you communicate to others about what you can do.

LinkedIn can be a great source of work for a freelancer. But the way you present yourself on the platform can mean the difference between standing out and getting ignored. So once you know who you are and what you want, make sure you present yourself to the world that way.

First of all, you need to define your title clearly in your LinkedIn headline or your website.

To do that, you must avoid two things.

1. Avoid pumping up your credentials to look good on LinkedIn. Like a post I came across called *The LinkedIn Effect*. You probably have seen it before, but if not, here is the general idea:

Someone who is a Recruiter in real life, presents himself on his LinkedIn profile as: 'Innovation Head Hunter, Visioner of the Potential, Career Enabler, Talent Exporter, EMEA.'

A Salesman in real life presents himself as 'Sales Manager, Area Director, Pro-Client Area Director, Passionate Solution-Delivering Leader.'

A Supervisor defines herself as 'Regional Chief Leader, Solution Evangelist, Project Manager, Business Guru, Team Guiding Spirit.'

The post is about humor, but if you check LinkedIn often as I do, you will find profiles like those in your network. If you want to get hired often, avoid using strategies that call for humor.

2. Avoid using taglines in your profile. In case you are not familiar with it, here are some examples of taglines people use in their profiles:

"I just help companies grow"
"Digital world expert"
"Connecting the dots between companies"
"Tech Nomad"
"Innovation disruptor"

All the examples above may sound good in an ad, but they are useless in your LinkedIn profile because they can mean anything. Those taglines only confuse rather than help.

Your definition has to be clear because when recruiters look for freelancers, they look for an 'interior designer' or a 'graphic designer' or a 'creative copywriter', etc.

You can add a point of difference if you have a specialty. A couple of examples to inspire you:

Emma Williams presents herself online in this way:
Emma Williams
Graphic Design & Illustration

Emma is making a clear statement about herself: she is a graphic designer. Plain and simple. But she is also making a differentiation by telling us her specialty.

Another example could be:
Eric Robinson
Book Editor & Creative Writer

Eric is crystal clear. Besides offering book editing, he provides creative writing. He has an added value and a differentiator, and therefore he could get more opportunities and charge a higher amount than a standard editor.

Defining yourself will make your life easier. Sometimes finding a distinction is difficult. If this is the case, and if you see nothing interesting that sounds good enough, better state your role as it is, without decoration.

Another point to develop is your contribution paragraph. You can use this one in your LinkedIn description and your about section of your website.

Here are some key questions you have to answer to define your contribution as a professional:
1. What's your background and title?
2. What makes you different from others?
3. Why should I hire you?

As an example, I will use the contribution paragraph I currently use as a designer.

1. What's your background and title?
I am a conceptual Art Director specialized in Graphic Design and brand development for digital, print or spatial design.

2. What makes you different from others?
Being pragmatic at heart, I love creating brands with strong and powerful ideas that are easy to understand by consumers, without compromising high-end aesthetics. On the other hand, I am also one of those that can spend days looking at fonts to find the right typography – some people say I am a bit of a nerd.

3. Why should I hire you?
I have worked on global projects that call for Art Direction, Graphic Design, and Spatial Design in the fields of fashion, luxury, culture, food, and music.

What I do:
Concept Creation
Design/Art Direction
Branding (Strategy and Design)
Installation, Spatial Design
Digital and Web Design

There are many ways to write this. I just used my example, but I am not telling you to follow it. You could write more or less. It depends on your experience and your way of expressing yourself. I just gave you a little guideline.

How you contribute is a critical point to have in your portfolio, because it is part of your identity and the reason why a company should hire you and not someone else. I got offered freelance assignments or full-time jobs because of that description. I got emails from recruiters saying: "Alex, I have a role and your description fits perfectly with what they are looking for."

Keep this in mind. Many recruiters or companies will read your description, so better be prepared.

It's important to be concise with your profile. A company will hire you as a specialist, so avoid presenting yourself with a broad spectrum of skills in the freelance department, or you could end up being disappointed about not finding your place, or you could make a company waste their time which will give you a bad reputation.

Presenting your work

If there is one thing that can make you look professional and worth your value, it is a proper presentation of your work.

Designers usually don't enjoy doing these much. I used to be like that too. To me, it was already enough to have thought and designed something. But actually, it isn't.

Having a brilliant project but not being able to sell it can be frustrating. So to avoid disappointments, make sure you reserve time to present it nicely, both to a client in the form of a presentation, or on your website as part of your portfolio.

PRESENTING YOUR WORK TO A CLIENT.

I have been working in top agencies where the presentations were done as if no one gave a shit. Hard to believe, but it happens that way. People don't realize the importance of presenting design work. You can't sell design or branding, and then showcase it as if you had no idea what design is.

You have to put more effort into presenting your work than in the work itself. Because you could have a mediocre idea, but if it's well explained, and it looks professional, it will be easier to sell than if not.

I present concepts, brands, photo shoots, packaging, websites and everything in between in my presentation template. Anything I present goes in a document, where I explain what I have done and why. I go through the presentation multiple times until it makes sense for someone who doesn't know anything about the project. That is, making the presentation easy to understand and pleasant to look at.

When the presentation is well done, it means to clients that you care about your work and about their needs. It says that you have empathy and you are a good communicator. They will think it was worth to hire you only by seeing a few slides of your presentation.

I have been complimented almost everywhere I have been about the way I present my work. The last thing someone told me was: "I have never seen anyone put so much effort into presenting an idea. You are making everyone look bad in this office."

The thing is, although it may look like you put a lot of effort, it is not time-consuming, and it helps you present your work in a way people will understand. You will also create anticipation, and the way you alternate slides to send your message can help to generate excitement.

I only spent some time creating one template, and for every new project I am doing, I use that template. It's drag and drop, or copy and paste.

And one important note: eliminate clutter.

Some people tend to make long-ass presentations, with a lot of irrelevant content. My advice is to be emphatic and keep in mind that people only have limited attention. Make it short and on point. Avoid a lot of text and explain it with images. Presentations have to be visual and told as a story.

A presentation deck has to be done in a way that anyone can understand it without you being present. These presentations will go around the company, so it needs to be 'idiot-proof'. The more slides and more content you try to put in, the more blurred it will get. The clearer you make it, the more time you will have to discuss in person and get instant feedback. Here, less is really more.

Put more effort into presenting your work than in the work itself.

PRESENTING YOUR WORK ONLINE.

No need for me to say this, you already know that you have to invest most of your time in your portfolio, and the way you present your work says a lot about you.

People struggle with this. They want to include everything they have done. But again, it's not about quantity; it's all about quality. It's about the work that speaks to you and your values.

Fundamental questions to consider: to whom is my portfolio directed? Who is my target? Random clients, recruiters or Creative Directors, who can potentially hire me?

Also, there is the question: should I always show the final result of a commission? This is the question I got asked the most about freelancing.

Not necessarily: use whatever you think was the best solution to that specific project and leave it as a proposal on your site, because they will hire you for your talent, not for the actual project you were involved in. The final result is not usually the best solution. After many changes and opinions are taken into account during the approval rounds, the final result can be a watered-down, suboptimal version of an original, better idea.

Nowadays, it's relatively easy to present your work nicely. There are plenty of good mockup templates that can be bought at a low cost and make your work shine at its best. Your work should be easy to understand and pleasant to look at; there is no need to try to re-invent, the work should speak for itself.

I suggest avoiding photographing your print work unless you have a photography studio and plenty of time to do it. For small price, you could save hours of valuable time and get stunning, photographic-quality mockups.

Also, have some empathy for the viewers. Make it easy for them and don't bore them to death with a dozen irrelevant pictures of your amazing work. If a picture doesn't add anything new, remove it. If they already got that piece of information earlier, there's no need to repeat it.

If you have your portfolio ready, social networking can help more than you can imagine. Share your site as much as you can - really, you never know. I've gotten jobs through Facebook and LinkedIn out of the blue. Contact websites that showcase creative work show them what you do, and they might feature your work. This will give you exposure and the more your name is out there, the more chances you will have.

**Fixed
quotes
backfire.
Quote
hourly.**

Quoting

Fixed quotes backfire. Quote hourly.

In my first project as a freelancer, I gave the advertising agency a day rate, thinking that was the usual thing to do. No one warned me about the possible consequences of doing so. And I ended up working 17 hours the first day, 12 hours the second and another 12 hours each day of the weekend. It was a horrible starting lesson; I worked 17 hours extra that no one paid me for.

Right after that gig, I started to quote hourly with no exceptions.

If you work for individual clients, a fixed quote might backfire for two main reasons:

First, the total amount can seem too expensive for them, and they might come up with some story for you to reduce your price.

And second, you will end up working overtime, as I did. You will probably work double the time that you estimated at first because there are always rounds of changes, and sometimes these changes take longer than expected. Since your client is paying for a result, they will feel free to be demanding, asking for changes or modifications until they are happy.

The problem with this dynamic is that you will lose enthusiasm, and the project will become tedious. Your only purpose at this point will be to finish the job. And the fastest way to achieve this would be to do what the client asks. Situations like this cause the roles to shift - the client becomes the designer, and the designer becomes a production machine. If you let this happen, you run the risk of the client losing trust in your expertise and asking you to try this and that, but not being content with anything. This is a lose-lose situation for everyone. Remember that although the client knows the problem, they don't necessarily know what the best solution is from the creative perspective. That's why you were hired.

If you work for a fixed price and you come up with the solution earlier than the expected time frame, you'll feel pressure to fill up your presentation with content that has no purpose, because you have to justify the original quote in the eyes of the client.

If you work for a company, again a day rate will backfire, because you will end up working overtime and not getting paid for it. If you sign a contract where it states your fixed day rate, you will have to deliver no matter what, even if it takes the whole day and night to finish your task. Agencies don't care much about your free time. For them, you are a freelancer who has a great life and who came to help them, and since you have a 'day' rate, it literally means that it can take the whole day.

When, instead, you choose to quote hourly, your clients will value your time more than anything, because they are paying for it. They will become more aware of what changes and corrections mean, they will deliver content more accurately, and they will pay more attention to details than ever before.

You should see the difference between a brief offered by a client for a fixed quote, and a brief by a client who is paying hourly - it's quite big. In the fixed quote case, you get more or less an idea of what's expected, but they hope you to work your magic. They pay less attention to the information they give you; they are less precise which makes you work more.

When you charge by the hour, briefings are usually so much more complete and well done. Often, there are almost no questions to ask. In this case, the meetings and presentations are also more efficient, and the client takes time to make a list of changes or modifications; the client actually gets involved in the project. Quoting hourly is the healthier option on every level.

But what if the client says they only have 'x' amount of money? This is a question I get asked very often. The answer to that is still the same: work hourly.

For instance, If your client says they only have €700 to do some social media, and you charge €70 an hour, that will make ten hours of work. So you must tell your client that they will get ten hours of your work with that budget, and also, to clarify what they can expect for it. And remember, if you must negotiate; negotiate what you will deliver - and not your price.

Approaching companies

Now that everything is ready and your work can be found on social networks as well as your personal site, it's time to share your work with companies who could potentially hire you. It is vital that you move and don't wait for openings or people to call you: there are no openings as a freelancer. They have to know about you and your work.

Once you have a list of the companies you would like to introduce yourself to, it's important to study the company's work before sending any emails. Make sure you have a reason to approach them, so look at what they do and explain in your email why you can be a great addition to their team.

Note: Unsolicited applications are underrated. To me, they have always been the most effective way of finding work. The fact that you apply and praise a company out of the blue shows your genuine interest, and they will appreciate your initiative and kind words.

To give you some inspiration, a little story of an unsolicited approach that worked well for me a few years ago.

A few years ago, I went to Stockholm to work as a freelancer at a well-known design studio. I loved the city, the company offered a free delicious lunch, and my apartment was right in the center of everything. All seemed perfect, but the job I was doing was not too exciting. So I decided to take my chances and look for other work in Stockholm, to see if I could stay longer or come back to the city.

I spent a couple of weekends researching and making a list of studios I would like to work for. This is always complicated when you are in another country. I didn't know where to start except Google. After a long while, I made a list of a few companies I was interested in. I went through their websites, I paid attention to the 'About' page and the work section, looking for a project or a piece of content I could appreciate.

Finally, I found a studio that did a project I found fascinating, and I took it as the starting point of my communication with them. I wrote them an email praising them for the fantastic work, and I explained why I liked it so much. In the end, very politely and subtly, I suggested grabbing a coffee, since I am a designer and I was in town for a few weeks, although I understood he could be busy, so no pressure at all.

They were not looking for people, they had no intention of hiring anybody, their studio was complete, and they were busy. I pressed the 'send' button, not expecting anything in return. I was due to return to my home city anyway.

A few hours after I sent the email, someone got back to me:

Hey Alex,

Thank you for your kind words about our work, I am happy to hear that. I was very involved in that project from scratch, so it is like my baby, and even though it was done some time ago, I still love it.

I also saw your website, and I like your work too. What you did in the window display section is impressive. Our company is expanding to do more of those projects, so I am interested in having a coffee, would you like to come by tomorrow?

It was the Creative Director of the company. I was lucky.

We ended up having lunch together, and we clicked very well. He wanted to hire me in a few months time to work on some of their new clients. I was lucky to reach him with that email, but it's all a matter of numbers. At least, even if it doesn't work and no one gets back to you, you know you have done your best from your side. The rest is just luck and coincidence.

So, what was so compelling about that email? How can you make yourself interesting to a company?

The key is understanding what drives people. Everyone's favorite topic is themselves, their achievements and their lives. So, to get a company interested in what you have to say, start by saying why you are so excited about them. You must do some work and research about them beforehand, of course. Read about the company and find something you find interesting about them. It could be something you read on the news, on their blog or just in the 'About' section of their website.

Now that you understand this fundamental detail, the formula for your cover letter or email should be:

1. Introduce yourself briefly
2. Praise them with something you found interesting or worth mentioning
3. Explain why you could be a good addition to their team
4. Say "thank you"

Here is an example as a reference:

Hello there at [Company XXX]

My name is Alex, and I just came across your article 'why designers should study business' on LinkedIn. I found the article to be inspiring and I decided to check your work as a company.

Your branding and window display design work motivated me to write this email. I didn't know your company designed the Christmas Windows at Harrod's, one of the most interesting displays I have seen in years. Brilliant idea and execution.

I like your work a lot, so I am taking this opportunity to briefly introduce myself and share my portfolio, as I think I could be a good fit in case you need extra help. I am a conceptual graphic designer with a background in brand development in digital, print and spatial design. I am also a bit of a nerd when it comes to typography ;)

I leave my portfolio here: www.alexaraez.com

* I believe you are busy and probably not looking for anyone at the moment, but If your time allows I would love to meet for a coffee and see if we could work together in the near future.

Thank you in advance for your time,
Alex

This is all you have to do to introduce yourself to a company.

You can write more or less if you feel like doing so. Everything can be improved in the letter above, but that is a basic structure that contains all the ingredients you need to be interesting for any company.

* If the company is looking for someone, remove the last paragraph and make sure to adapt your cover letter or email.

Letting them find you

It might be common sense. Maybe you could even skip this chapter altogether. But if your web and email addresses don't include your name, perhaps you should keep reading.

Imagine I am a recruiter at a big agency. And all of a sudden, someone asks me to find a freelance designer urgently. The project is important, and the freelance designer must start today or tomorrow the latest. The project is long-term, the budget is generous, and the client is a good one to have in any portfolio.

I would have a list of freelancers somewhere stored in my contact list. But I don't remember what each of those freelancers was good at. I am looking for someone specific. And out of the blue, I remember one person who would be the perfect fit. Imagine that person is you.

This would be a great freelance assignment. You will work at a big company, for a nice brand, and you will get paid at your highest rate. The ideal freelance project, you are the perfect person, and you are available. Perfect match.

I search for your website and email address, but I can't find you. I keep typing names and looking into my contacts, but your name doesn't show. How come? I remember this person perfectly. After a while, I give up and try someone else. I send a couple of emails, and after some back a forth, I finally manage to hire someone else instead of you. Damn it, your perfect opportunity is now gone, and you don't even know why. Right?

When using your email or web address, avoid anything that is not professional or not your name. The email account you found profound or funny does not work here, this is about being practical. I work with email regularly and sometimes I need to contact someone to ask a question or to even hire for a project. I never remember their email addresses, I type their name, and they will show up. But a couple of my contacts' email addresses don't include their names; they just wanted to be different. And they succeeded, they are different. The problem is that this is not the place to be creative, here it should be easy for others to find you. Do you think I spend any time remembering their addresses? I'd instead contact and hire someone else.

If your name is Emma Williams, your email address must be emma.williams@email.com. If that name is already taken, use a similar one, or add your city at the end.

If you don't want to leave room to miss any opportunities, better use a professional address. One that makes it easy for anyone to find you in Outlook or contacts list.

Recruitment agencies

There is no discussion about what's the best way for a freelancer to get hired: directly from companies or clients, without any middleman.

But what If you have been desperately looking for work and no one hires you? What if you want to work for a big brand, but you never manage to contact the right person?

As a freelancer that has been dealing with good years and bad years, I suggest keeping all doors open.

I can't understand why many freelancers avoid working with recruiters. I get it; they get a cut from a salary that could be yours. It sucks, it is you the one who commutes to the company and works eight hours a day. But, what's the point of avoiding recruiters when you are not getting any work?

I got hired once by a brand most people would like to have in their portfolio thanks to a recruiter, and it was the longest assignment I ever got. It was for about two years. Without him, I wouldn't have been able to get hired.

Working with recruiters only gives you more opportunities. And it doesn't mean you have to work only with them; you can always work by yourself for other companies. You can also decline offers by saying you are not available. It is ok; they have more people to offer the assignments to.

I met a brilliant designer once who had come to Amsterdam to do an internship.

He took the internship because he thought it was the only way to start a career here when he already had real experience. He was even a bit popular within the design community.

During his internship, he looked for a real job so he could extend his stay. But despite all his talent, he found nothing. Some studios didn't even get back to him, while others just offered a coffee. But nothing work-related came out of it. He got tired of the whole situation and left the country to try his luck somewhere else.

At that time I was working full-time at a communications agency. But one year after I was hired, some legal issues arose, and all of a sudden, the owners announced that the company would close due to bankruptcy. We were all out of a job.

That same day, a colleague of mine told me to check something out. He sent me a link to a 'creative recruitment agency' in the city. Something I had never heard of in my entire life. All this time, I had been doing all of it on my own. Making the common mistakes every job searcher makes.

The creative recruiters are the ones who search for the right talent and put them in contact with the company; they also negotiate their salaries or their hourly rates. So the creatives get the job they like, the company finds what they are looking for, and the recruiter gets a cut of it - everybody wins.

In the three years I had spent in the city desperately looking for a decent job, no one had told me this - no one. From all the designers and professionals I met, I just needed one to say: "hey, try a recruitment agency." It could have been as simple as that. I always wondered: did they know or were they clueless about this too?

It might not work for everybody, but my experience with recruitment agencies has been nothing but great. Was it luck? Maybe. My first time working with one of them was great. They helped me to raise my value, they improved my CV and got me in contact with big names. They didn't work with small studios; they were there only for big clients, the first division - no joke.

When they got me an interview with a big fashion firm, it took just one meeting to get the job, and they negotiated my salary to almost double of what I was making at the small agency.

They told me that I was being too cheap and undervaluing myself, that I had so much to offer and that a small company wouldn't get me far.

When I told a friend of mine this story, he got very upset. He had been in the city for four months looking for a job and found nothing, even though he was one of the few talented ones. The same reaction from an ex-colleague of mine: "why the hell has no one told me that before?" I gave him the agency's business card, he met with them, and within a short time, he was hired for several freelance projects. It worked for him, too.

I explained to my recruiters my own job-hunt story, and they were surprised as well - they said: "what? You have been looking on your own for three years, and you made it this far?"

My first recruiter was pretty good. She was a getting a cut, yes. But I wouldn't have gone so far without her help. She also got me my first freelance assignment. And again, for one of the biggest tech agencies worldwide. A name that looks good on your profile.

One last note: there are also bad recruiters out there, watch out for those. There are so many recruiters desperately 'hunting' on LinkedIn, that don't even pay attention to read your profile. They send generic emails to everyone. Don't waste time with these people; it only creates anticipation for something that won't happen. They are just creating a big resources list, but most likely they won't give you anything. These people work on commission, so watch out when negotiating your salary or rates. It may look like they are helping you, but they are putting their interests first.

Big brands

If you come from a small company, in which budget and resources are limited, switching to a big one might seem like walking into Disneyland.

Companies at the top level have the privilege of hiring the best professionals; people with great talent who deliver in high-pressure situations and tight deadlines. They do their work on a big scale, and the production process is pretty amazing. That also means that, by working there, you might get international exposure. Plus, you get to meet and share projects with the very best. The experience you can get from it is invaluable.

Once you step into that world, the people with whom you collaborate will treat you like a professional. They will respect your decisions since they know that you got there for a reason. The fact that you worked with the best will open doors to go anywhere, and it will give you the same credibility as winning an award.

Put it this way:
You are at a networking event with a lot of potential clients.
They know little or nothing about the creative industry, but they might need your professional skills for their businesses at some point.
You tell them that you are a designer (or the like).
They ask what you've done or what your specialties are.
You tell them that you did a particular project and you won a Red Dot Award.
They don't know what you are talking about.

If instead of that, you tell them you have worked for a company like Nike, they will say, "oh that's nice! What did you do?" Hearing familiar brand names helps them relate to what you do and gives you credibility.

And this will help you tremendously in the future, especially being a freelancer.

I got hired several times by agencies that didn't interview me. They saw the client list, and they only asked for my availability and rates. That with just one well-known brand name in my profile.

Although don't set your expectations too high about the work you will do for them. Usually, these brands have strong teams that they want to maintain. The internal team will get the best creative work, while you, as a freelancer, are there to help. Sometimes, it is good to do executional work without much thinking involved. I believe it is good to step into all the shoes of the creative work chain.

All the freelancers I know agree that having a known brand in your profile does more to your career than any other achievement.

Big brands give you credibility.

Scarcity

We like your work, although we are not looking for anyone at the moment. But we would like to keep you in our freelance pool for future projects.

That was the email I got the most in 2016.

—

A friend of mine started working as a freelancer a few years ago, and he hasn't stopped since then. As a freelancer, if you work so often, you could save up quite a bit of money. And you should, because not everyone is like my friend.

I did pretty well in my first three years; I had a good balance of work and free time. It was wonderful. But I don't know what happened in 2016, that my luck plummeted and I almost got no work. I worked in total around nine weeks. The rest was free time.

I did enjoy the first month not going to work, but after that, I spent serious time and effort looking for work, even in other countries. The bank account was going down the hill, so was my confidence. I started to doubt myself. I changed my website, updated my portfolio and tried to publish some previous work.

I still got the same email about going to the freelance pool. I probably ended up in all freelance pools available.

It was only at the end of the year when I started using social media to promote my work. I learned a thing or two about those channels, and I decided to give it a try. I became quite active in those networks, and I started to get hits. My work was being commented on and shared often. I used LinkedIn to announce my availability without looking desperate or needy.

After about two months of consistently posting two or three times a week, I finally got in contact with a recruiter who offered me a good and long-term assignment. Exactly what I needed.

That year was the worst in my freelance career. And you, as a freelancer, must be willing to pass through a year like that, and even worse. Which means two things:

Be sure to quote keeping in mind that you don't have the stability others have.

Be smart about how you spend money. If you like the freelance life, you won't want to go back to a 9-to-5 job. So having a savings plan is your best bet to have a long-lasting career.

Be prepared for times of abundance and times of scarcity. A freelance career is one of risk, but it gives you the freedom full-time jobs don't.

ASAP

I left everything I was doing. I blocked my precious weekend to work on it. I felt a bit stressed about it all, I was busy as hell, but I had to help the friend of my friend to create his brand identity and be able to launch "ASAP," as he said.

I used to get stressed anytime someone would ask me to design something for them. It seemed that everyone was in a hurry to launch their businesses or products. I always wondered if that was the nature of the design industry. To do things fast to meet deadlines and never the miss the train of success.

I thought that all that rush meant that, perhaps – in my positive way of believing everyone knew what they were doing – the project, brand, album cover, book jacket, marketing campaign... and everything in between, was going to hit a particular prime time which will make the company sell millions and become an absolute success.

The truth is that no one really knows what they are doing. There is no train for success, special prime time or a real deadline. It's all in their heads. Yes, there are deadlines and event dates, and better times than others to launch certain things. But usually, the ones who hit the prime time and do this well are the big corporations, and these companies plan things and don't leave everything for the last minute.

Small businesses and startups are not great at planning, and whatever they ask you will be probably needed yesterday.

And here, is where you should protect yourself. Protect yourself against their bad planning and self-created urgency.

The friend of my friend, the one I spent my weekend helping with his branding, needed the project yesterday. I wasn't sharp enough, and I didn't increase my rate.

I didn't ask for company details to invoice either. It was all based on trust.

I delivered. He had his branding done and ready to be used by Monday.

A week went by, and I didn't hear from him.

"What the fuck?" – I thought.

I wrote him an email asking for feedback. He got back to me: "Looks great Alex, let's talk about the website and other applications, I want this ASAP so I can launch soon."

"ASAP again?" – I asked myself.

I said it was no problem, but I was swamped, and I couldn't focus on the site at this moment. I asked him his details to invoice him for the part we agreed at first. He told me he was registering the business and getting back to me in a few days.

Weeks went by again, and I heard nothing.

Months went by, and I heard nothing.

Six months went by, and I lost my patience. I asked him again, and he got back telling me he was having issues in his relationship. Like I care.

Then I remember a scene of the movie The GoodFellas. The one about how they accepted no excuses. "Fuck you, pay me."

I said I was sorry for him, but I needed to send the invoice. I finally sent it, and my accountants made sure I got paid.

I put myself under stress. I worked on my precious weekend. I delivered my work for a project that was needed ASAP.

F* YOU,**

PAY ME.

Six months and still there was no website, no logo and no business.

I have many stories like this, but you get the point. If your clients are in a rush and want things yesterday, an excellent way to solve this – and test if it is true – is to tell them that tight deadlines come with a price. Most likely they will step back, but if not, there is a second way to protect yourself: give them homework.

Tell them to deliver the information (or whatever takes them some effort) in a way it will be clear to you what to do. And once you have that, then you will be able to start. Without it, you won't move a finger.

This will show you if they are serious. And if not, you know the drill.

The startup promise

Subject: Opportunity

Hey Alex, My name is Emil, I am the head of the marketing department of the national group Acme Nutrition. We specialize in the research of target audiences and focus on offering the best quality service to our customers.

Therefore Branding and Packaging are important tools in getting recognition for our products.

We saw your website, and we think your profile could fit our product's needs. We are working on a new line of sports drinks that will sell in supermarkets all over Europe.

We will need:
Branding
Naming
Packaging
Merchandising
Communications

If you fit our criteria and you are willing to collaborate with us in the form of partnership share in our business, you could be part of Acme Group and develop more projects with us in the future. Let us know if you would like to be part of this great and fast-growing company.

Regards,
Emil

Whether you've been in the field for a long time or are just starting out, you might know that in the journey of becoming a creative you may encounter many 'great, fast-growing companies' offering you the real deal.

Start-ups will start filling your mailbox with requests for your services in exchange for more work in the future. Single entrepreneurs will offer you a big cut once the product does well in the market. Your neighbor that just opened a shop will ask you to design some stuff for him, etc.

All this sounds amazing when you are not familiar with the reality of it. You keep telling your friends and family that you are busy and have a lot of work. You tell them enthusiastically that companies are offering you shares in their fast-growing business, and so on.

Although it can bring you good things for your portfolio, you keep being broke and you don't learn that much with these kinds of projects. These work-now-we-will-pay-later strategies work well with designers because they sell the idea of growth and belonging. "Grow with us," they say.

The truth is that they are asking you to work for free in exchange for nothing. Really, nothing.

You won't get a higher salary in six months, and you won't get paid for future work – if there is any at all. First, a company with any decency will have the money to pay a professional. Second, if they are growing that fast, how come they don't invest in what matters to the business?

Perhaps I have been too long in the business. Or maybe I encountered too many cheap people who promised 'the dream' and delivered little.

I believe cheap clients bring you cheap outcome, professionally and financially. People who want you to work for free – or pay you with candy – don't respect all the years you invested in your profession.

Avoid free work based on promises of growth or more work in the future, as this will make you work for expectations. And when nothing happens, you will end up disappointed. Do free work only if you want to, and when you know you will enjoy it and use it for your portfolio.

When the people who ask you for free work are genuine and

appreciate your effort, you will feel their honesty. If instead, they are selling you some bullshit about opportunities and long-term business ideas for the future, you'd better save your energy and look for real work instead.

What Emil was asking me in that email was to create their entire brand identity and all the products associated with it, a job worth several thousands of euros, and a job that will take months to be developed and finished. In exchange, he offered me promises.

When in doubt about these emails, remove the clutter out of it to get to what they are actually saying. Sometimes it is just too ridiculous to be believed.

Quality, not quantity

When I was in design school, I used to think branding projects were a pain in the ass.

We were told that branding was the most challenging assignment a designer can encounter; therefore we were given plenty of time to develop them.

But I always wondered, what if you come up with a great idea right from the start? What do you do with the rest of the time?

Having so much time means that you have to fill it with content, with sketches, printouts, explorations, research… all to justify your given time and the work produced. I used to hate making 'memoirs,' I always did them in the end, making it all up.

This same thing happens with assignments in the real world. I believe that the longer you have, the longer it will take. If your time is restricted, you will spend time doing what is important because the clock is running. And what is more important happens at the beginning, when the concept of the project needs to be defined.

Agencies often get tight deadlines, especially in the advertising world. And sometimes, they manage to create great ideas out of little time. Is that because stress helps? Not really. I believe it's because there is no room for clutter, fillers or a dozen meetings in between – there's only room for what's necessary.

In an 'ideal' deadline - where the time given might be longer than usual - agencies or freelancers need to prove that they did a lot of work to justify the original quote. The client gets a deck with a lot of slides and a good story. It might look like a week of work, but probably took about one or two days.

I have seen presentations of projects where the studio/agency had plenty of time. They presented four branding proposals, none of them with a well-defined concept, and the executions were so poor that the client refused to work with them again. It makes sense: if you present four ideas, it means that you as a company are not standing for anything in particular, and you are unsure of your criteria.

Sometimes just one or two good ideas, well presented, will work better than anything else. The client sees that you are standing up for something and that you are confident to defend it without any bullshit or fillers. Sometimes, even a sketch is more efficient than a poor render, because it lets the client imagine something. They might even appreciate it more, since they feel involved in the creation process.

I have also seen agencies that are efficient when it comes to presentations. In about ten slides, they present the branding concept, the architectural approach, and the design direction. Just one concept and one design direction. Straight to the point, and everything made sense. Most of the time, these people end up getting the job, with only a little feedback.

The advantage of working this way is that the client sees the conceptual direction first with no sketches. Just the strategy and mood boards, so both client and designer can be on the same page. I never saw these people presenting several ideas. Only one, or two at most.

I believe in this way of working, and that's how I do it with my clients, as well. Depending on the subject, I ask an average of two days to come up with a conceptual approach of just one good idea (two ideas if I am exceptionally inspired). The client sees where I am going before I even open the design software. This way, the client can first imagine the possibilities of a concept. Something we creatives do easily, but clients don't.

If we can get our client as excited as we are with an idea, it will be one of those nice projects we both will be proud of.
At this phase and with this process, there isn't any massive presentation with a lot of slides and ideas, just the bare necessities. I don't need to

justify anything, and the client knows it because it is an open process based on time.

The saying is true. It's not about quantity; it's about quality.

Case in point: Paula Scher, a partner at Pentagram, came up with the idea for the Citi Group (of Citibank fame) logo on a napkin. It took her seconds to draw it, but nearly 32 years of experience to learn how to do it. That's why Citi paid her $1.5 million to create a logo from that napkin sketch.

There is no need to justify your knowledge. When the best solution is the one right front of your eyes, why not use that one?

Just enough is more.

Milton Glaser

Skinny dogs, bad taste and relationships.

If you are a designer who enjoys working on your own terms and when you want, you'll need to learn how — and when — to reject a project.

Many times, I made the mistake of accepting everything, ending up drowning in work and having no life.

As a freelancer, it's important to keep your options open and be able to choose in case a better, more exciting project comes your way. But even more important is to keep an eye on who you work for and what your stress levels are.

Over the years, I learned to follow my instincts. Even if the work looks promising, I need to meet in person with the client. To me it is all about values and respect. Those come first, work comes second.

There are a few things I look into to spot what might be a bad client:

UNCLEAR BRIEFS AND DIRECTIONS.

If before starting the project, things are unclear or the client is not communicating clearly, red flag.

A disorganized client can make your life miserable, and make you feel like you're working with the client forever. People who are not clear are usually the ones who change their minds constantly. They also like to promise and don't deliver, which can make the project endless. You will get information and feedback bit by bit, making you work five minutes today here, ten minutes next week there, on and on until nothing gets finished. You won't get paid until the work ends –unless you negotiate your hourly rate and agree on sending weekly invoices – and this will drive you mad because you probably want to move on and get the project finished.

"THIS IS AN OPPORTUNITY FOR YOU…"

When a client tries to manipulate you with phrases like that, red flag.

Cheap clients are the worst. This is what my father always warned me about business: "Skinny dogs attract fleas."

Cheap clients are incredibly demanding. For them, whatever they are paying you means a fortune to them. It's like they are paying you with their own blood. They don't understand the value of what we do, they are insecure, they don't trust you, and they don't respect you at all.

WHEN THEY HAVE A LOT OF IDEAS.

Be careful with these. These are the ones who are frustrated creatives who made the wrong choice when they were younger.

They think they still have the talent, and this particular idea is what will make them reach the stars. Or if it doesn't work, then this other idea. Or this one. Or that one.

People who want you to make their ugly ideas come true should get a technical designer, not a creative freelance designer who is in this business to make a living.

"I KNOW EXACTLY WHAT I WANT."

People with big egos are easy to handle, do what they want and praise them for their 'spectacular' vision. If you need money and they pay well, pick your battles and do whatever they need.

I avoid these people, because it's hard for me to waste my valuable time working for someone I dislike.

I enjoy working for good people who respect others. I want to feel good when I receive a phone call from my client. I want to be happy to meet that person for a coffee. I want to be excited and wanting to show them the work I have done. I want to be able to 'tell it like it is' to them. That's the only rule. I want to feel good in all aspects of the relationship.

Clients are relationships to be built with people you like, so choosing them carefully is a skill worth having.

Skinny dogs attract fleas.

Part three
—
CHOOSHING YOUR ELEPHANTS

"It isn't for me."

A friend of mine decided to go freelance after eight years at the same company. He wanted a new challenge and tried the adventure of going solo. He was fortunate and managed to find work quickly. He was also updating his LinkedIn any time he would find work at another new company. It seemed he was doing great in such a short time.

A few months after the success, he went back to the same company, this time as a Creative Director.

"It wasn't for me," he told me once. All the networking, looking for work every week. Sending emails and updating his portfolio was a bit much and too intense. He preferred the stability of just going to an office, getting paid at the end of the month and not having to do anything else.

"It's not for everybody," I told him. Being a freelancer is not about having a portfolio and being connected. It's a business, and you have to work to make it worth all the time. You have to find work, you have to do your administration, you have to be sure to get paid on time, and on top of all those tasks, you have to be a designer. You have to create, present and sell your work to clients.

Being a freelancer is more work than being full-time, although if done correctly, it can bring you a career on your terms. Which is what we all want after all.

"I can't go back to a full-time job anymore."

Another friend of mine needed a fresh start after burning out. I invited her to try freelancing. She was talented and had a strong character, I thought it could work for her. She was indecisive for a long time, but after two failed full-time jobs, she decided to give it a try.

She now tells me how much she is enjoying it, working on her terms, having to report to no one and doing what she likes doing. She works throughout the week as she pleases. She is doing beautiful work, and she is getting a good reputation. She has now partnered with another freelancer to work together.

"The best decision I have taken in my professional life," she tells me.

Choose your elephants

The truth is, neither corporate teams nor the freelance life are a guarantee of smooth sailing. Both come with their own elephants, and you'll have to navigate them.

Whichever path you choose, your health and happiness should be your top priority. The choice to work yourself into a burnout for a company that doesn't respect or value you is no choice at all. And the easiest way to kill your motivation and creativity is to surround yourself with people who force you to work in conditions that set you up for failure. Or for clients who expect outstanding work for intern prices.

We all have to pay our dues. Every job isn't going to be perfect. In fact, I suspect that you already recognize more than one of the situations I described in this book. And trust me, you'll encounter many more of them. But when you do, remember that it's an Elephant Under the Rug.

You can be part of changing the industry for the better. You can learn to protect yourself and others when you see situations like this. You can do your part to ensure that you're not encouraging or allowing the behaviors that can affect your health and well-being.

It's our responsibility to educate others about how we work and what we value, and dealing appropriately with the issues that only harm the industry are the first steps to a more exciting and fulfilling career, for us, and the ones that come after us.

Your two cents

The next edition of this book is there to be written, and I invite you to add your two cents.

If you have a story to share, any comments or feedback about the book, I would gladly read it and implement it. You can email me at contact@alexaraez.com.

I want to help people avoid burnouts, I want to help people take the risk and leave companies with no values. I also believe the industry can change for the better, little by little. If you feel the book can help others to wake up and take the next step in the career, or just make some people laugh, you can help tremendously by leaving a review on amazon.com. Reviews are what make people trust in the author and the quality of the book. That's probably why you bought this book, too.

Thank you again for your time, and I wish you all the best with your career!

Keep me posted,
Alex

Milton Keynes UK
Ingram Content Group UK Ltd.
UKHW010311220224
438247UK00004B/462